How to Start and Grow a Transportation Business

Do You Aspire to Be a Transportation Entrepreneur?

Here's Your Guide

Content

- Finding the Right Employees
- Training Your Drivers

Chapter 8: Developing Your Operations

- Establishing Routes and Schedules
- Implementing a Dispatch System

Chapter 9: Building Your Reputation

- Developing a Strong Brand Identity
- Creating a Strong Online Presence

Chapter 10: Marketing and Advertising

- Building Your Customer Base
- Utilizing Social Media

Chapter 11: Customer Service

- Providing Excellent Service
- Resolving Customer Complaints

Chapter 12: Pricing Strategies

- Setting Your Rates
- Understanding Your Costs

Chapter 13: Managing Your Fleet

- Keeping Vehicles in Good Condition
- Tracking Maintenance and Repairs

Chapter 14: Record Keeping

Chapter 1.   Introduction

Welcome to the exciting world of transportation business! This chapter is designed to provide a comprehensive introduction to the transportation industry, and give you an overview of what it takes to start and run a successful transportation business. We understand that starting a new business can be an intimidating process, but with the right knowledge and resources, you can be well on your way to creating a successful venture.

Understanding the Transportation Industry

Transportation is a crucial part of our daily lives. From getting to work, to delivering goods, to traveling for leisure, transportation plays a vital role in our daily routines. The transportation industry encompasses a wide range of services, including taxi and ride-sharing, bus and shuttle services, trucking, and freight and logistics. No matter the size of your operation, the goal of any transportation business is to provide reliable and efficient services to customers.

Why Start a Transportation Business

Starting a transportation business can be a lucrative and rewarding venture. The demand for transportation services is growing, and with the right combination of skills, resources, and determination, you can build a successful business. Additionally, the transportation industry offers a high degree of flexibility, allowing you to choose the type of services you want to offer, and the hours you want to work. Whether you're looking to start a small side hustle, or build a large-scale operation, the transportation industry offers endless opportunities for growth and success.

In conclusion, the transportation industry is a dynamic and constantly evolving sector, offering endless opportunities for entrepreneurs. With the right combination of skills, resources, and determination, you can build a successful transportation business that provides valuable services to your customers, and generates significant income for you and your family.

Stay tuned for the next chapter where we will delve into market research, and explore how to analyze the competition, and understand your target market.

Chapter 2.   Market Research

So, you've decided to take the plunge and start a transportation business. Congratulations! Now, it's time to get to work and do some research to ensure that you're entering the right market, and offering the right services to your customers. In this chapter, we'll be diving into the importance of market research, and exploring how you can gather the information you need to make informed decisions about your business.

Why Market Research is Essential

Market research is a critical step in the process of starting a transportation business. It provides valuable information about your target market, competition, and industry trends, allowing you to make informed decisions about your business. By conducting market research, you can determine the viability of your business idea, and identify any potential challenges or obstacles you may face.

Where to Start with Market Research

The first step in conducting market research is to define your target market. This will help you determine who your customers are, and what their needs and preferences are. You can conduct market research by surveying potential customers, analyzing industry data, and conducting competitive analysis.

Once you've defined your target market, you can start exploring the competition. This will help you understand what services are currently being offered, and how you can differentiate yourself in the market. You can gather information about your competition by conducting online research, attending industry events, and speaking with industry professionals.

Finally, it's important to stay up-to-date with industry trends and changes. This will help you identify opportunities for growth and innovation, and stay ahead of the competition. You can gather information about industry trends by attending conferences and trade shows, reading industry publications, and monitoring online forums and social media.

Putting Your Market Research to Work

Once you've gathered all of your market research information, it's time to put it to work. This information will be essential in developing your business plan, determining the services you want to offer, and setting your pricing strategy. Additionally, your market research will help you identify any potential challenges or obstacles you may face, and provide you with the information you need to overcome them.

In conclusion, market research is an essential step in the process of starting a transportation business. By conducting market research, you'll be able to make informed decisions about your business, and ensure that you're offering the right services to your customers. In the next chapter, we'll explore the importance of developing a business plan, and how it can help you achieve success in your transportation business.

Chapter 3.   Business Plan Development

So, you've done your market research, and you're ready to take the next step in starting your transportation business. Now it's time to develop a comprehensive business plan. A business plan is a roadmap for your business, outlining your goals, strategies, and the steps you need to take to achieve success. In this chapter, we'll be diving into the importance of business plan development, and exploring how you can create a plan that will help you reach your business goals.

Why a Business Plan is Essential

A business plan is essential for any new business, and it's especially important for a transportation business. A business plan provides structure and direction, helping you to stay focused and on track as you build your business. Additionally, a business plan is essential for securing financing, as lenders and investors will want to see a clear and well-thought-out plan for your business.

Components of a Business Plan

A comprehensive business plan should include the following components:

1. Executive Summary: A brief overview of your business, including your mission statement, goals, and key strategies.

2. Market Analysis: An overview of your target market, competition, and industry trends. This section should include information from your market research.

3. Service Offerings: A description of the services you'll be offering, and how they meet the needs of your target market.

4. Marketing and Sales Strategy: A plan for promoting your business and attracting customers, including advertising, marketing, and sales strategies.

5. Operations Plan: A description of your day-to-day operations, including the resources you'll need, and the processes you'll follow.

6. Financial Projections: A detailed financial plan, including your start-up costs, revenue projections, and break-even analysis.

7. Appendices: Additional information and supporting documents, including resumes, licenses, and contracts.

Creating Your Business Plan

Creating a business plan can be a daunting task, but it's important to take the time to develop a comprehensive plan that outlines your goals and strategies. There are several ways to create a business plan, including hiring a consultant, using a business plan template, or developing a plan on your own. Whichever method you choose, make sure that you take the time to research and gather the information you need to create a comprehensive and well-thought-out plan.

In conclusion, a business plan is an essential component of starting a transportation business. It provides structure and direction, and helps you stay focused and on track as you build your business. By taking the time to create a comprehensive and well-thought-out business plan, you'll be well on your way to achieving your business goals and building a successful transportation business. In the next chapter, we'll explore the steps you need to take to secure financing for your business.

Chapter 4. Legal Considerations

Starting a transportation business comes with its share of legal considerations, and it's important to be aware of these considerations from the outset. In this chapter, we'll be exploring the legal requirements you need to be aware of when starting your transportation business, including registering your business, obtaining the necessary licenses and permits, and protecting your business with insurance.

Registering Your Business

The first step in starting your transportation business is registering your business with the appropriate government agencies. This typically involves choosing a business structure, such as a sole proprietorship, partnership, limited liability company (LLC), or corporation, and registering your business with the appropriate state agencies. It's important to research the different business structures to determine which one is right for your business, and to seek the advice of a lawyer or accountant if necessary.

Obtaining Licenses and Permits

Once you've registered your business, you'll need to obtain the necessary licenses and permits to operate your transportation business. This may include obtaining a commercial driver's license, as well as permits for operating your vehicles, such as a commercial vehicle permit and a motor carrier permit. Additionally, you may need to obtain licenses for the specific type of transportation services you'll be offering, such as a taxi or limousine service license. It's important to research the specific requirements for your business and to seek the advice of a lawyer or accountant if necessary.

Insurance

Insurance is a critical component of any transportation business, as it protects your business from potential liabilities. You'll need to obtain liability insurance for your vehicles, as well as insurance for your drivers, if applicable. Additionally, you may need to obtain workers' compensation insurance for your employees, and cargo insurance for the goods you'll be transporting. It's important to research the different types of insurance available, and to work with an insurance broker to determine the best coverage for your business.

In conclusion, starting a transportation business involves a number of legal considerations, including registering your business, obtaining the necessary licenses and permits, and protecting your business with insurance. It's important to be aware of these legal requirements from the outset, and to seek the advice of a lawyer or accountant if necessary. In the next chapter, we'll explore the importance of developing a marketing and sales strategy for your business.

Chapter 5.   Choosing Your Fleet

When starting a transportation business, one of the most important decisions you'll make is choosing your fleet. The type of vehicles you choose will impact your business's operational costs, efficiency, and reputation, so it's essential to choose wisely. In this chapter, we'll be exploring the different options available for building your fleet, and the factors to consider when making your decision.

Types of Vehicles

When it comes to choosing your fleet, you have several options, including cars, vans, buses, and trucks. The type of vehicle you choose will depend on the type of transportation services you plan to offer, as well as your budget and operational requirements. For example, if you're starting a taxi or limousine service, you may choose to purchase a fleet of cars or vans, while if you're starting a trucking business, you'll need to choose a fleet of trucks.

Factors to Consider

When choosing your fleet, there are several key factors to consider, including:

1. Operating costs: The cost of operating your vehicles will impact your business's bottom line, so it's important to choose vehicles that are fuel-efficient, reliable, and low-maintenance.

2. Capacity: The capacity of your vehicles will impact your ability to transport goods or passengers efficiently, so

it's important to choose vehicles that are appropriately sized for your business needs.

3. Comfort and safety: The comfort and safety of your vehicles will impact your reputation as a transportation provider, so it's important to choose vehicles that are well-equipped, safe, and comfortable for your customers.

4. Technology: The technology in your vehicles, such as GPS and telematics, will impact your operational efficiency, so it's important to choose vehicles that are equipped with the latest technology.

5. Maintenance and repairs: The maintenance and repair costs of your vehicles will impact your business's bottom line, so it's important to choose vehicles that are reliable and low-maintenance.

Leasing vs. Owning

Once you've considered the factors listed above, you'll need to decide whether to lease or own your fleet. There are pros and cons to both options, and the choice you make will depend on your budget, business goals, and personal preference.

For example, if you're starting a new transportation business and don't have the funds to purchase a fleet of vehicles outright, leasing may be the best option for you. Leasing allows you to spread the cost of your fleet over time, and eliminates the risk of depreciation. However, leasing also means that you won't own your vehicles outright, and may limit your ability to make modifications to your fleet as needed.

On the other hand, if you have the funds to purchase a fleet of vehicles outright, owning your vehicles may be the best option for you. Owning your vehicles gives you complete control over your fleet, and eliminates the costs associated with leasing. However, owning your vehicles also means that you'll be responsible for all costs associated with maintenance, repairs, and depreciation.

In conclusion, choosing your fleet is a critical component of starting a transportation business, and the type of vehicles you choose will impact your business's operational costs, efficiency, and reputation. When choosing your fleet, consider factors such as operating costs, capacity, comfort and safety, technology, and maintenance and repairs. Decide whether to lease or own your fleet based on your budget, business goals, and personal preference. In the next chapter, we'll explore the importance of developing a marketing and sales strategy for your business.

Chapter 6.   Financing Your Business

Starting a transportation business requires a significant amount of capital, and financing your business is an important part of the process. In this chapter, we'll explore the various financing options available to you, and help you determine which option is best for your business.

Sources of Financing

When financing your transportation business, there are several options available, including:

1. Personal savings: Using your own personal savings is one of the simplest ways to finance your business, and allows you to retain complete control over your business.

2. Bank loans: Bank loans are a common source of financing for small businesses, and are typically used to finance large expenses, such as the purchase of vehicles or real estate.

3. Venture capital: Venture capital is a type of investment that provides financing in exchange for equity in your company. This type of financing is typically used by high-growth startups, and is usually only available to businesses that have already achieved some level of success.

4. Government grants: Government grants are a form of financing that does not need to be repaid, and are

typically provided for specific purposes, such as research and development or job creation.

5. Crowdfunding: Crowdfunding is a type of financing that involves raising capital from a large number of individuals, usually via an online platform. Crowdfunding is typically used for smaller amounts of financing, and allows you to build a community of supporters for your business.

Factors to Consider

When choosing a source of financing for your transportation business, there are several factors to consider, including:

1. Interest rates: The interest rate you'll be charged will impact your monthly payments and overall cost of financing, so it's important to choose a financing option with a competitive interest rate.

2. Repayment terms: The repayment terms of your financing will impact your monthly payments and overall cost of financing, so it's important to choose a financing option with terms that are manageable for your business.

3. Collateral requirements: Some financing options require you to put up collateral, such as your home or other assets, as security for the loan. If you're unable to repay the loan, your collateral may be seized, so it's important to choose a financing option that does not require collateral.

4. Ownership: Some financing options may impact your ownership of your business, such as venture capital or equity financing, so it's important to choose a financing option that allows you to retain control over your business.

In conclusion, financing your transportation business is an important part of the process, and there are several options available, including personal savings, bank loans, venture capital, government grants, and crowdfunding. When choosing a source of financing, consider factors such as interest rates, repayment terms, collateral requirements, and ownership. In the next chapter, we'll explore the importance of developing a marketing and sales strategy for your business.

Chapter 7.   Hiring and Training Your Team

As your transportation business grows, you'll need to hire and train a team of employees to help you manage operations and provide exceptional service to your customers. In this chapter, we'll explore the process of hiring and training your team, and provide tips on how to build a strong and motivated workforce.

Hiring Your Team

When hiring employees for your transportation business, it's important to choose individuals who are aligned with your values and mission, and who have the skills and experience necessary to help your business succeed. Here are some tips for hiring your team:

1. Define your job requirements: Before you start the hiring process, it's important to clearly define the job requirements for each position you're looking to fill. This will help you attract the right candidates, and ensure that you're hiring individuals who are well-suited for the role.

2. Use a thorough interview process: Your interview process should be thorough, and should include multiple rounds of interviews, skills assessments, and reference checks. This will help you identify the most qualified candidates, and ensure that you're hiring individuals who are a good fit for your business.

3. Offer competitive compensation: To attract the best candidates, it's important to offer competitive

compensation and benefits packages. This will help you retain top talent, and ensure that your employees are motivated and engaged in their work.

Training Your Team

Once you've hired your team, it's important to provide them with the training they need to be successful in their roles. Here are some tips for training your employees:

1. Provide comprehensive onboarding: Your onboarding process should be comprehensive, and should include both job-specific training and an overview of your company's values and mission. This will help your employees understand what's expected of them, and ensure that they're fully prepared for their roles.

2. Offer ongoing training and development opportunities: To help your employees grow and develop, it's important to offer ongoing training and development opportunities. This can include in-person training sessions, online courses, and mentorship programs.

3. Encourage open communication: Encouraging open communication between employees and managers will help build a strong and motivated workforce. This can include regular team meetings, one-on-one discussions, and opportunities for employees to provide feedback and suggestions.

In conclusion, hiring and training a team of employees is an important part of growing your transportation business. When hiring your team, it's important to choose individuals who are aligned with your values and mission, and to use a thorough interview process to identify the best candidates. When training your employees, it's important to provide comprehensive onboarding, offer ongoing training and development opportunities, and encourage open communication. In the next chapter, we'll explore the importance of developing and maintaining strong relationships with suppliers and customers.

Chapter 8. Developing Your Operations

Developing a well-functioning operations plan is crucial for the success of your transportation business. In this chapter, we'll explore the key components of a strong operations plan and provide tips on how to develop and implement effective processes and procedures.

Defining Your Operations Strategy

Your operations strategy should be tailored to meet the unique needs of your transportation business and should be informed by your business plan and market research. Here are some key considerations when developing your operations strategy:

1. Identify your target market: Understanding your target market will help you determine the types of transportation services you should offer, the areas you should focus on, and the type of fleet you'll need to meet customer demands.

2. Determine your operational processes: Defining your operational processes is an essential part of your operations strategy. This should include how you'll manage your fleet, handle customer requests and payments, and resolve any operational issues that may arise.

3. Consider your operational needs: Consider your operational needs, including the number of vehicles you'll need, the types of vehicles you'll need, and the level of maintenance and support you'll require.

Implementing Your Operations Plan

Once you've developed your operations strategy, it's time to implement it. Here are some tips for putting your operations plan into action:

1. Develop a detailed schedule: A detailed schedule will help you stay on track and ensure that your operations are running smoothly. This should include when and how you'll acquire vehicles, how you'll manage maintenance, and when you'll start accepting customers.

2. Establish efficient processes and procedures: Establishing efficient processes and procedures will help you manage your operations effectively, and ensure that you're providing a consistent and high-quality service to your customers.

3. Monitor and adjust as needed: Regularly monitoring your operations and making adjustments as needed is an important part of maintaining a well-functioning operations plan. This includes tracking performance metrics, seeking feedback from employees and customers, and making changes as needed to improve operations.

In conclusion, developing a strong operations plan is crucial for the success of your transportation business. When developing your operations strategy, it's important to consider your target market, operational processes, and operational needs. Once your operations strategy is in place, it's important to implement it by developing a detailed schedule, establishing efficient processes and procedures, and monitoring and adjusting as needed. In the next chapter, we'll explore the importance of marketing and promoting your transportation business.

Chapter 9.   Building Your Reputation

Your reputation is one of the most valuable assets of your transportation business. A positive reputation can lead to increased customer loyalty, more business referrals, and overall growth for your company. In this chapter, we'll explore how to build and maintain a strong reputation for your transportation business.

Establishing Trust with Your Customers

Establishing trust with your customers is essential to building a strong reputation. Here are some key strategies for building trust with your customers:

1. Deliver on your promises: If you promise to arrive at a certain time, make sure you do. If you promise a certain level of service, make sure you deliver. Delivering on your promises will help establish trust with your customers.

2. Be transparent: Be transparent with your customers about your business practices and procedures. This includes things like how you handle customer complaints, how you manage customer information, and how you handle payment transactions.

3. Provide excellent customer service: Providing excellent customer service is essential to building a strong reputation. This includes responding promptly to customer inquiries, being helpful and friendly, and resolving customer issues quickly and efficiently.

Building Your Online Reputation

In today's digital age, your online reputation is just as important as your offline reputation. Here are some strategies for building a positive online reputation for your transportation business:

1. Claim your online profiles: Make sure you have a presence on popular online platforms, such as Facebook, Twitter, and LinkedIn. This will help you build a following and connect with customers and potential customers.

2. Respond to reviews: Responding to customer reviews, both positive and negative, is an important part of building a strong online reputation. Responding to negative reviews in a professional and helpful manner can help turn a negative experience into a positive one.

3. Share positive content: Share positive content, such as customer testimonials and success stories, on your online profiles and website. This will help promote your business and build a positive reputation online.

Maintaining Your Reputation

Maintaining a strong reputation is just as important as building one. Here are some strategies for maintaining a strong reputation for your transportation business:

1. Continuously evaluate and improve your customer service: Regularly evaluate your customer service and make improvements as needed. This will help maintain

a high level of customer satisfaction and help build your reputation over time.

2. Stay engaged with your customers: Stay engaged with your customers by regularly communicating with them and responding to their inquiries. This will help build a relationship with your customers and help maintain a strong reputation.

3. Be proactive about managing negative experiences: Be proactive about managing negative experiences and responding quickly and efficiently to resolve any issues that may arise. This will help minimize the impact of negative experiences and help maintain a strong reputation.

In conclusion, building and maintaining a strong reputation is essential for the success of your transportation business. By establishing trust with your customers, building a positive online reputation, and continuously evaluating and improving your customer service, you'll be well on your way to building a strong reputation for your business. In the next chapter, we'll explore the importance of pricing and pricing strategies for your transportation business.

Chapter 10. Marketing and Advertising

Marketing and advertising are crucial elements of any successful transportation business. Without effective marketing and advertising strategies, your business may struggle to attract and retain customers, even if you offer the best service and prices in the market. In this chapter, we'll explore how to develop and implement marketing and advertising strategies for your transportation business.

Developing Your Marketing Plan

A marketing plan is a critical component of your overall business plan. It outlines the steps you'll take to promote your business and reach your target customers. When developing your marketing plan, consider the following:

1. Who is your target market? Understanding your target market will help you determine the best marketing strategies to reach them.

2. What are your marketing goals? Identifying your marketing goals will help you determine which marketing strategies will best help you achieve them.

3. What are your marketing budget and resources? Knowing your budget and available resources will help you determine the best marketing strategies to pursue.

Advertising Your Business

Advertising is one of the most effective ways to reach your target customers and promote your transportation business. Here are some advertising strategies to consider:

1. Online advertising: Online advertising, such as Google AdWords and Facebook Ads, can be a cost-effective way to reach a large number of potential customers.

2. Local advertising: Local advertising, such as print and online classifieds, can be an effective way to reach potential customers in your area.

3. Networking and word-of-mouth: Networking and word-of-mouth are two of the most effective forms of advertising. Encourage your satisfied customers to refer others to your business and participate in local networking events.

Marketing Your Business

Marketing your business involves promoting your brand and attracting new customers. Here are some marketing strategies to consider:

1. Content marketing: Content marketing involves creating and sharing valuable content to attract and retain customers. This can include blog posts, videos, and social media posts.

2. Influencer marketing: Influencer marketing involves partnering with influencers to promote your business. This can be a cost-effective way to reach a large number of potential customers.

3. Public relations: Public relations involves building relationships with media outlets and journalists to promote your business and build your brand.

In conclusion, marketing and advertising are critical components of any successful transportation business. By developing a marketing plan, advertising your business, and marketing your business, you'll be well on your way to reaching your target customers and growing your business. In the next chapter, we'll explore the importance of customer service and how to provide excellent customer service to your customers.

Chapter 11. Customer Service

Customer service is one of the most important aspects of running a successful transportation business. Your customers are the backbone of your business, and providing them with excellent customer service will not only help retain them, but also attract new customers through positive word-of-mouth. In this chapter, we'll explore the importance of customer service and how to provide excellent customer service to your customers.

The Importance of Customer Service

Customer service is the foundation of any successful business, and the transportation industry is no exception. Providing excellent customer service can help you:

1. Build trust and loyalty with your customers: Trust and loyalty are key to retaining customers and attracting new ones. By providing excellent customer service, you'll build trust and loyalty with your customers.

2. Increase customer satisfaction: Satisfied customers are more likely to recommend your business to others and continue to use your services.

3. Improve customer retention: Customers who receive excellent customer service are more likely to stick around, which will reduce your customer acquisition costs and improve your bottom line.

4. Improve your reputation: A positive reputation can help you attract new customers and build your brand.

Providing Excellent Customer Service

Providing excellent customer service requires a commitment to your customers and a focus on their needs. Here are some tips for providing excellent customer service:

1. Listen to your customers: Listen to your customers and understand their needs. This will help you better meet their needs and provide better customer service.

2. Be responsive: Respond to your customers promptly and be available when they need you.

3. Be empathetic: Put yourself in your customers' shoes and understand their perspective. This will help you provide better customer service.

4. Be proactive: Anticipate your customers' needs and take steps to meet them before they ask.

5. Follow up: Follow up with your customers after each interaction to ensure their needs were met and they are satisfied.

Training Your Team

Training your team on the importance of customer service and how to provide excellent customer service is critical to the success of your business. Here are some steps to take when training your team:

1. Teach your team the importance of customer service and how it affects the success of the business.

2. Provide customer service training, including role-playing exercises, to help your team develop the skills they need to provide excellent customer service.

3. Set expectations for customer service and hold your team accountable for meeting them.

4. Reward and recognize your team members who provide excellent customer service.

In conclusion, customer service is a critical aspect of running a successful transportation business. By providing excellent customer service, you'll build trust and loyalty with your customers, increase customer satisfaction, improve customer retention, and improve your reputation. In the next chapter, we'll explore the importance of pricing and how to set competitive prices for your transportation services.

Chapter 12. Pricing Strategies

Setting the right prices for your transportation services can be a challenging task, but it's essential to the success of your business. In this chapter, we'll explore the different pricing strategies you can use for your transportation business and how to set competitive prices that will help you grow your business and increase your profits.

The Importance of Pricing

Pricing is a critical aspect of running a successful transportation business. Setting the right prices can help you:

1. Attract new customers: Competitive prices can help you attract new customers who are looking for affordable transportation services.

2. Increase profits: By setting competitive prices, you'll increase your profits and improve your bottom line.

3. Improve customer satisfaction: Customers who receive affordable transportation services are more likely to be satisfied with your services.

4. Compete in the market: By setting competitive prices, you'll be able to compete with other transportation businesses in your market.

Pricing Strategies

There are several pricing strategies you can use for your transportation business, including:

1. Cost-plus pricing: Cost-plus pricing involves adding a markup to your costs to determine your prices. This strategy is straightforward, but it may not always result in the most competitive prices.

2. Value-based pricing: Value-based pricing involves setting prices based on the value your customers receive from your services. This strategy takes into account the unique benefits of your services and helps you set prices that are competitive and profitable.

3. Competitor-based pricing: Competitor-based pricing involves researching your competitors and setting your prices based on their prices. This strategy helps you remain competitive in your market.

4. Volume-based pricing: Volume-based pricing involves offering discounts for customers who purchase a large volume of your services. This strategy helps you attract customers who need transportation services regularly and increase your profits.

Setting Competitive Prices

When setting competitive prices for your transportation services, there are several factors you should consider, including:

1. Your costs: Your costs, including fuel costs, maintenance costs, and driver costs, will impact the prices you can set for your services.

2. The market: The prices in your market will impact the prices you can set for your services. Research your

competitors to determine what prices they are charging for their services.

3. Your target customer: The prices you set will also be impacted by your target customer. Consider what your target customer is willing to pay for your services.

4. The value of your services: Consider the unique benefits and value of your services when setting your prices.

In conclusion, pricing is a critical aspect of running a successful transportation business. By using a combination of pricing strategies and considering the factors mentioned above, you'll be able to set competitive prices that will help you grow your business and increase your profits. In the next chapter, we'll explore the importance of technology and how technology can help you streamline your transportation business.

Chapter 13. Managing Your Fleet

Managing your fleet is a critical aspect of running a successful transportation business. In this chapter, we'll explore the different aspects of fleet management and how to effectively manage your fleet to ensure your business runs smoothly and efficiently.

What is Fleet Management?

Fleet management refers to the process of managing and maintaining the vehicles used in your transportation business. This includes tasks such as:

1. Vehicle maintenance: Keeping your vehicles in good working order, including regular maintenance and repairs.

2. Fuel management: Monitoring and controlling fuel costs, including tracking fuel consumption and usage.

3. Vehicle tracking: Tracking the location and usage of your vehicles, including monitoring speed, route, and fuel consumption.

4. Driver management: Managing and training your drivers, including ensuring they are qualified and following safety regulations.

The Importance of Fleet Management

Effective fleet management is essential for the success of your transportation business for several reasons, including:

1. Improved efficiency: By effectively managing your fleet, you'll improve the efficiency of your business operations, reducing downtime and maximizing profits.

2. Lower costs: Effective fleet management can help you reduce costs, including fuel costs, maintenance costs, and vehicle replacement costs.

3. Improved safety: By properly maintaining your vehicles and training your drivers, you'll improve the safety of your transportation services and reduce the risk of accidents.

4. Increased customer satisfaction: Customers who receive safe and efficient transportation services are more likely to be satisfied with your services.

Strategies for Effective Fleet Management

There are several strategies you can use to effectively manage your fleet, including:

1. Implementing a vehicle tracking system: A vehicle tracking system can help you monitor the location and usage of your vehicles in real-time, improving your fleet management and reducing costs.

2. Regular vehicle maintenance: Regular vehicle maintenance is essential for keeping your vehicles in good working order and reducing maintenance costs.

3. Driver training and management: Properly training and managing your drivers can improve their performance and reduce the risk of accidents.

4. Fuel management: Monitoring and controlling fuel costs can help you reduce fuel costs and improve your bottom line.

In conclusion, managing your fleet is a critical aspect of running a successful transportation business. By using the strategies mentioned above, you'll be able to effectively manage your fleet, improve the efficiency of your business operations, and increase your profits. In the next chapter, we'll explore the importance of technology and how technology can help you streamline your transportation business.

Chapter 14. Record Keeping

Record keeping is an important aspect of any business, and the transportation industry is no exception. In this chapter, we'll explore why record keeping is essential for the success of your transportation business and the different types of records you should keep.

Why is Record Keeping Important?

Record keeping is essential for the success of your transportation business for several reasons, including:

1. Legal compliance: Keeping accurate records is essential for complying with tax laws and regulations.

2. Financial management: Keeping accurate records is essential for managing your finances and making informed decisions about your business.

3. Improved efficiency: By keeping accurate records, you'll be able to easily access the information you need to make informed decisions about your business, improving the efficiency of your operations.

4. Problem solving: Keeping accurate records can help you identify and solve problems in your business, improving your bottom line.

Types of Records to Keep

There are several types of records you should keep for your transportation business, including:

1. Financial records: Financial records include financial statements, invoices, receipts, and other financial documents related to your business.

2. Vehicle records: Vehicle records include information about your vehicles, including maintenance records, fuel consumption, and repair history.

3. Driver records: Driver records include information about your drivers, including their qualifications, training, and performance.

4. Customer records: Customer records include information about your customers, including their contact information and history with your business.

How to Keep Accurate Records

Keeping accurate records is essential for the success of your transportation business. Here are a few tips to help you keep accurate records:

1. Use a system: Using a computerized record-keeping system can help you keep accurate records and easily access the information you need.

2. Train your employees: Make sure your employees understand the importance of keeping accurate records and provide them with the training they need to do so.

3. Regularly update your records: Regularly update your records to ensure they are accurate and up-to-date.

4. Store your records securely: Store your records securely to protect them from theft or loss.

In conclusion, record keeping is an important aspect of the success of your transportation business. By keeping accurate records, you'll be able to comply with tax laws and regulations, manage your finances, improve the efficiency of your operations, and make informed decisions about your business. In the next chapter, we'll explore the importance of insurance and how insurance can protect your transportation business.

Chapter 15. Insurance Considerations

Insurance is an important aspect of protecting your transportation business. In this chapter, we'll explore the different types of insurance you should consider for your business and how insurance can protect your business from potential risks.

Why is Insurance Important for Your Transportation Business?

Insurance is important for your transportation business for several reasons, including:

1. Protection from financial loss: Insurance can protect your business from financial losses in the event of an accident, theft, or other unforeseen circumstances.

2. Legal compliance: Some types of insurance are required by law, and failure to have the required insurance can result in fines and other penalties.

3. Peace of mind: Having insurance can give you peace of mind, knowing that your business is protected in the event of a loss.

Types of Insurance to Consider

There are several types of insurance you should consider for your transportation business, including:

1. Auto liability insurance: Auto liability insurance is required by law and covers damages to third-party property and people in the event of an accident.

2. Commercial auto insurance: Commercial auto insurance covers damages to your vehicles and is typically required for businesses that operate vehicles for commercial purposes.

3. General liability insurance: General liability insurance covers damages to third-party property and people and is typically required for businesses that interact with the public.

4. Workers' compensation insurance: Workers' compensation insurance covers the medical expenses and lost wages of employees who are injured on the job.

How to Choose the Right Insurance for Your Business

Choosing the right insurance for your transportation business can be a challenge, but there are several factors you should consider when making your decision, including:

1. The type of business you operate: Different types of businesses require different types of insurance, so it's important to choose insurance that is appropriate for your business.

2. The potential risks associated with your business: Assess the potential risks associated with your business and choose insurance that covers those risks.

3. Your budget: Consider your budget when choosing insurance and choose insurance that provides the coverage you need at a price you can afford.

4. Your insurance needs: Consider your insurance needs and choose insurance that provides the coverage you need for your business.

In conclusion, insurance is an important aspect of protecting your transportation business. By choosing the right insurance, you can protect your business from financial losses, comply with the law, and have peace of mind knowing that your business is protected. In the next chapter, we'll explore the importance of keeping up with industry trends and staying competitive in the transportation industry.

Chapter 16. Safety and Compliance

Safety and compliance are two important aspects of running a successful transportation business. In this chapter, we'll explore the importance of maintaining safety in your operations and complying with the regulations that apply to your business.

Why is Safety Important in Transportation?

Safety is important in transportation for several reasons, including:

1. Protection of your employees and customers: Maintaining safety in your operations helps to protect your employees and customers from harm.

2. Legal compliance: Safety regulations are often required by law, and failure to comply with these regulations can result in fines and other penalties.

3. Protection of your vehicles: Maintaining safety in your operations helps to protect your vehicles from damage, which can result in costly repairs and downtime.

4. Protection of your business: Maintaining safety in your operations helps to protect your business from liability in the event of an accident.

How to Ensure Safety in Your Operations

To ensure safety in your operations, there are several steps you should take, including:

1. Develop a safety policy: Develop a safety policy that outlines the procedures and guidelines for maintaining safety in your operations.

2. Train your employees: Train your employees on the safety policies and procedures for your business.

3. Regularly inspect and maintain your vehicles: Regularly inspect and maintain your vehicles to ensure that they are in good working condition.

4. Comply with regulations: Comply with all relevant safety regulations, including those related to vehicle maintenance and operation.

5. Respond to accidents: Develop a plan for responding to accidents and have procedures in place for responding to accidents if they occur.

Why is Compliance Important in Transportation?

Compliance is important in transportation for several reasons, including:

1. Legal compliance: Compliance with regulations is required by law, and failure to comply with these regulations can result in fines and other penalties.

2. Protection of your business: Compliance with regulations helps to protect your business from liability in the event of an accident or other incidents.

3. Protection of your employees and customers: Compliance with regulations helps to protect your employees and customers from harm.

How to Ensure Compliance in Your Operations

To ensure compliance in your operations, there are several steps you should take, including:

1. Stay informed: Stay informed about the regulations that apply to your business and regularly review them to ensure that you are in compliance.

2. Hire knowledgeable staff: Hire staff that has knowledge of the regulations that apply to your business and ensure that they are trained on these regulations.

3. Have systems in place: Have systems in place for ensuring compliance, such as regular inspections and audits.

4. Respond to incidents: Have a plan in place for responding to incidents, such as accidents or regulatory violations, and respond promptly to any incidents that occur.

In conclusion, safety and compliance are two important aspects of running a successful transportation business. By maintaining safety in your operations and complying with the regulations that apply to your business, you can protect your business from liability, protect your employees and customers from harm, and ensure the success of your business. In the next chapter, we'll explore the importance of managing your finances and keeping your business financially healthy.

Chapter 17. Technology and Innovations

Welcome to chapter 17, where we'll be discussing the exciting world of technology and innovations in the transportation industry. It's a rapidly changing landscape and it's important to stay on top of the latest advancements to ensure the success of your business.

From GPS tracking and fleet management software, to alternative fuel options and self-driving vehicles, there are a multitude of ways technology is changing the way we operate and manage our transportation businesses. The benefits are numerous, from increased efficiency and cost savings, to improved safety and customer satisfaction.

One of the biggest technological advancements in the industry is the rise of GPS tracking and fleet management software. These tools allow you to monitor your vehicles in real-time, providing valuable insights into vehicle location, speed, fuel consumption, and maintenance needs. This information can help you optimize routes, reduce fuel costs, and minimize vehicle downtime.

Alternative fuel options are also becoming increasingly popular in the transportation industry. From electric vehicles to biofuels, there are a number of environmentally-friendly options to consider when choosing your fleet. Not only are these options better for the environment, they also have the potential to reduce operational costs, as alternative fuels are often less expensive than traditional gasoline or diesel.

Another exciting development in the industry is the rise of self-driving vehicles. While this technology is still in its infancy, it has the potential to revolutionize the way we think about transportation. Imagine being able to send a self-driving vehicle to pick up a customer, or to deliver a shipment, without having to worry about the cost of a driver or the potential for human error. The possibilities are endless!

In conclusion, technology and innovation play a crucial role in the success of a transportation business. Whether you're just starting out or you're looking to expand your operations, it's important to stay on top of the latest advancements and make use of the tools and technologies that can help you streamline your business and stay ahead of the competition.

Chapter 18. Fuel Management

Fuel is one of the biggest expenses for any transportation business, and managing it effectively can mean the difference between profit and loss. In this chapter, we'll take a closer look at fuel management and the steps you can take to keep your costs under control.

One of the first things to consider when it comes to fuel management is the type of fuel you're using. As mentioned in Chapter 17, alternative fuel options like electric or biofuels are becoming increasingly popular, and can often offer significant cost savings compared to traditional gasoline or diesel. But it's important to consider the upfront cost of switching to alternative fuels, as well as the availability of charging or fueling stations in your area.

Another important aspect of fuel management is monitoring and optimizing fuel consumption. GPS tracking and fleet management software can help you track your vehicles' fuel consumption in real-time, and can even provide insights into how you can reduce consumption by optimizing routes, reducing idling time, or encouraging more efficient driving habits.

It's also important to regularly check your fuel prices and shop around for the best deals. Some gas stations may offer discounts for volume purchases, so if you're a large transportation company, it may be worth considering setting up a bulk purchase agreement with a supplier.

In addition to reducing fuel costs, there are also tax incentives and government programs available for companies that are using alternative fuels or improving fuel efficiency. These can include tax credits, grants, and other financial incentives, so it's worth exploring the options in your area.

In conclusion, fuel management is a critical component of any successful transportation business. By considering the type of fuel you're using, monitoring fuel consumption, shopping for the best prices, and taking advantage of tax incentives and government programs, you can keep your fuel costs under control and ensure the long-term success of your business.

Chapter 19. Cost Control

Starting and growing a transportation business can be a costly venture, and it's important to have a solid plan in place for managing your expenses. In this chapter, we'll take a closer look at cost control and the strategies you can use to keep your costs under control.

One of the first things to consider when it comes to cost control is budgeting. Having a realistic and detailed budget will help you keep track of your expenses and ensure you're not overspending. It's important to allocate funds for all the major expenses such as fuel, vehicle maintenance, insurance, employee salaries, and advertising, and to regularly review your budget to make sure you're on track.

Another key aspect of cost control is reducing waste. This can be achieved through a variety of means, such as reducing fuel consumption (as discussed in Chapter 18), reducing vehicle idling time, and streamlining operations to eliminate inefficiencies.

It's also important to shop around for the best deals when it comes to supplies and services. This includes everything from fuel to insurance, and from vehicle maintenance to marketing. Negotiating with suppliers and taking advantage of bulk purchasing deals can help you keep your costs down.

In addition, you can consider outsourcing certain services, such as bookkeeping or customer service, to reduce your overall costs. By outsourcing these tasks, you can free up time and resources to focus on growing your business, and you may also benefit from the expertise of professionals who have years of experience in these areas.

Finally, it's important to monitor your expenses regularly and make adjustments as needed. Regular financial statements and reports can help you keep track of your expenses and identify areas where you can reduce costs. By implementing cost control strategies and monitoring your expenses, you can ensure that your transportation business remains profitable for years to come.

In conclusion, cost control is an essential component of any successful transportation business. By having a solid budget, reducing waste, shopping for the best deals, outsourcing services, and monitoring expenses, you can keep your costs under control and ensure the long-term success of your business.

Chapter 20. Time Management

In any business, time is money, and in a transportation business, this is especially true. With multiple tasks to complete, customers to serve, and deadlines to meet, effective time management is crucial for success. In this chapter, we'll take a closer look at time management strategies that can help you streamline your operations and achieve your goals.

The first step to effective time management is setting priorities. It's important to know what needs to be done and when, and to prioritize tasks accordingly. This can be achieved through the use of a to-do list, project management software, or by simply prioritizing tasks based on their level of urgency and importance.

Another key aspect of time management is delegation. While it may be tempting to do everything yourself, delegating tasks to your team can help you save time and achieve more. When delegating tasks, it's important to be clear about your expectations and to provide your team with the tools and resources they need to succeed.

In addition, time management also involves avoiding distractions and staying focused on the task at hand. This means putting aside distractions such as social media, email, and other interruptions, and focusing on the most important tasks. By staying focused and avoiding distractions, you can complete tasks more efficiently and effectively.

Another effective time management strategy is to make use of technology. From dispatch software to GPS tracking systems, there are a variety of tools and technologies that can help you manage your time more efficiently. By automating certain tasks and streamlining your operations, you can free up time to focus on other aspects of your business.

Finally, it's important to take breaks and make time for yourself. While it may be tempting to work non-stop, taking breaks can actually help you be more productive and avoid burnout. Whether it's taking a walk, grabbing a coffee, or simply taking a few minutes to stretch, taking regular breaks can help you refresh and recharge, so you can be more productive when you return to work.

In conclusion, effective time management is an essential component of any successful transportation business. By setting priorities, delegating tasks, avoiding distractions, making use of technology, and taking breaks, you can manage your time more effectively and achieve your goals. With a focus on time management, you can streamline your operations, serve your customers better, and achieve success in your transportation business.

Chapter 21. Strategic Planning

As a transportation business owner, it's important to have a clear and well-defined plan for the future. Strategic planning allows you to set goals, determine the steps needed to achieve those goals, and allocate resources accordingly. It's like mapping out a journey – you need to know where you're going, how you're going to get there, and what you'll need along the way.

The first step in strategic planning is to assess your current situation. Take a look at your business operations, your finances, and your competition. What are your strengths and weaknesses? What opportunities and threats are you facing? This information will help you to determine your goals and objectives.

Once you have a clear picture of your current situation, it's time to set some goals. Be specific and realistic – what do you want to achieve in the short-term, mid-term, and long-term? It could be things like increasing your revenue, expanding your fleet, or improving your customer satisfaction.

Next, you need to determine the steps you'll need to take to achieve your goals. This could involve updating your business plan, investing in new technology, hiring more staff, or restructuring your operations. Make sure you have a clear timeline and allocate the resources you'll need to get there.

Finally, it's important to regularly review and adjust your strategic plan as needed. The transportation industry is constantly changing, and your plan should adapt to those changes. Keep an eye on your progress and make changes as necessary. If you're not meeting your goals, you may need to reassess your plan and make some changes.

Remember, a solid strategic plan is an essential tool for success in any business, but it's especially important in the transportation industry where there are so many variables at play. By taking the time to plan and stay focused, you'll be able to build a successful and sustainable transportation business.

Chapter 22. Networking

Networking is a crucial aspect of growing your transportation business. Building relationships with other businesses, suppliers, customers, and industry professionals can help you to expand your reach, find new opportunities, and gain valuable insights into the transportation industry.

One of the best ways to start networking is by attending industry events and conferences. These events provide a platform for you to meet and connect with others in the transportation industry. You can exchange ideas, share experiences, and make valuable connections that can help you grow your business.

Another great way to network is by joining professional organizations and trade associations. These groups offer educational resources, training opportunities, and access to a network of other transportation professionals. By getting involved with these organizations, you can stay up-to-date with the latest industry trends and developments.

Don't underestimate the power of personal connections. Take the time to get to know your suppliers, customers, and other business owners in your area. Attend community events, join local business organizations, and build relationships with others in your community. These personal connections can help you to build your reputation and find new opportunities for growth.

Finally, don't be afraid to ask for help or advice. Many people in the transportation industry are more than happy to share their knowledge and expertise with others. By reaching out to others, you can gain valuable insights and advice that can help you grow your business.

In conclusion, networking is an essential aspect of growing your transportation business. By building relationships and expanding your network, you can find new opportunities, stay up-to-date with industry trends, and gain valuable insights that can help you succeed. So get out there and start building your network today!

Chapter 23. Delegation

As a transportation business owner, it can be tempting to try to do everything yourself. After all, you want to make sure everything is done right, and you have a lot of responsibilities on your plate. But as your business grows, it becomes increasingly important to delegate tasks and responsibilities to others.

Delegation is the process of assigning tasks and responsibilities to others so that you can focus on the most important aspects of your business. By delegating effectively, you can free up time and energy, increase productivity, and improve the quality of your work.

So, how do you delegate effectively? Here are some tips to get you started:

1. Identify your strengths and weaknesses. Take a step back and assess your skills and abilities. What tasks do you excel at, and which ones do you struggle with? Knowing your strengths and weaknesses can help you to delegate effectively.

2. Hire the right people. When you are hiring new employees, look for individuals who have the skills and expertise you need to delegate effectively. Make sure you have a clear understanding of their strengths and weaknesses and that they have the necessary skills to take on the tasks you need to delegate.

3. Clearly define responsibilities. When delegating tasks, make sure you have a clear understanding of what

needs to be done and what the expectations are. Provide your employees with clear instructions, timelines, and any other information they need to complete the task effectively.

4. Provide support and resources. Your employees will need your support and resources to succeed in their tasks. Make sure you provide them with the necessary tools, resources, and training they need to complete their tasks effectively.

5. Communicate regularly. Regular communication is key to successful delegation. Make sure you check in with your employees regularly to provide feedback, answer questions, and provide support.

Delegation is a key aspect of growing your transportation business. By delegating effectively, you can free up time and energy, increase productivity, and improve the quality of your work. So start delegating today and watch your business grow!

Chapter 24. Employee Motivation

When it comes to running a transportation business, your employees are the lifeblood of your operations. They are the ones who are behind the wheel, handling the logistics, and making sure everything runs smoothly. It's essential to keep your team motivated and engaged, so they can provide the best possible service to your customers.

One of the best ways to motivate your employees is by recognizing their efforts and hard work. You can do this by offering bonuses, promotions, and incentives for meeting specific goals. When your employees feel valued, they are more likely to be motivated and invested in the success of your business.

Another way to keep your employees motivated is by providing them with the necessary tools and resources they need to perform their jobs effectively. This can include things like up-to-date software, equipment, and training. When your employees feel equipped to handle any challenge that comes their way, they will be more confident and motivated to do their best work.

You can also create a supportive and positive work environment that fosters collaboration and teamwork. Encouraging your employees to work together, share ideas, and support each other can help build a sense of community within your business. When your employees feel like they are part of something bigger than themselves, they will be more motivated to do their best work.

Finally, it's essential to communicate openly and honestly with your employees. This means taking the time to listen to their concerns, answering their questions, and addressing any issues they may have. When your employees feel like they are being heard and valued, they are more likely to feel motivated and engaged in their work.

In conclusion, keeping your employees motivated is crucial for the success of your transportation business. By recognizing their efforts, providing the necessary tools and resources, creating a supportive work environment, and communicating openly, you can ensure that your employees are motivated and invested in the success of your business.

Chapter 25. Diversity and Inclusiveness

As a transportation business owner, one of your top priorities should be creating a workplace environment that values diversity and inclusiveness. This means not only promoting diversity in the makeup of your employees, but also fostering a culture of respect, understanding, and open-mindedness.

In this chapter, we'll explore why diversity and inclusiveness are important for your business and how you can promote these values in your workplace.

The Benefits of Diversity and Inclusiveness

A diverse and inclusive workplace can bring a number of benefits to your business. For starters, having a diverse workforce can help you better understand and serve your customers. For example, if your employees come from different cultural backgrounds, they may be able to offer unique perspectives on how to reach and serve diverse customer groups.

Inclusiveness can also improve employee morale and motivation. When employees feel valued and respected, they are more likely to be engaged and committed to their work. This can lead to increased productivity, improved customer service, and higher levels of employee satisfaction and retention.

Creating a Diverse and Inclusive Workplace

To create a diverse and inclusive workplace, you need to start with a commitment to these values. This means setting policies and procedures that promote diversity and inclusiveness, as well as actively seeking out diverse candidates for your team.

It's also important to create a supportive work environment that encourages open communication, respect for others, and an understanding of different perspectives. This can include regular diversity and inclusiveness training for your employees, as well as a culture of active listening and feedback.

Finally, be sure to celebrate and recognize the contributions of all employees, regardless of their background. This can help reinforce the importance of diversity and inclusiveness in your workplace, while also promoting a sense of community and belonging.

In conclusion, promoting diversity and inclusiveness in your transportation business is not only the right thing to do, but it can also bring many benefits to your business. By being proactive and intentional in your approach, you can create a workplace that values and supports diversity and inclusiveness, and that will help your business thrive for years to come.

Chapter 26. Handling Competition

Starting a transportation business can be exciting, but it can also be challenging. One of the biggest challenges you'll face is competition. In any industry, there will always be competitors who are trying to do what you're doing, and sometimes they'll even be doing it better. But don't let this discourage you. Competition can be a good thing, it keeps you on your toes and pushes you to be better. In this chapter, we'll discuss how to handle competition and make your business stand out.

First, it's important to research your competition. Find out what they're offering, how they're doing it, and what they're doing differently than you. This information will help you understand what your customers are looking for and what they expect from your business. From there, you can create a unique selling proposition (USP) that sets you apart from the competition. Your USP is what makes your business different and why customers should choose you over the competition.

Next, focus on your strengths. What are you good at? What can you do better than your competition? Make sure to highlight these strengths in your marketing and advertising efforts. For example, if you have a strong commitment to safety, make sure your customers know it. If you have a state-of-the-art technology system, make sure your customers know that too.

In addition to focusing on your strengths, it's important to be flexible and adapt to the changes in the market. If your competition starts offering a new service or product, you may need to start offering it too. This doesn't mean you should blindly follow your competition, but it does mean you should be open to new ideas and changes that could help your business grow.

Finally, it's important to remember that competition is a natural part of doing business. Don't let it stress you out or discourage you. Instead, use it as motivation to be the best you can be. With hard work, determination, and a little bit of luck, you can make your transportation business a success, even in a competitive market.

In conclusion, handling competition is a critical aspect of starting and growing a transportation business. By researching your competition, focusing on your strengths, being flexible and adaptable, and using competition as motivation, you'll be well on your way to success.

Chapter 27. Diversifying Your Services

As your transportation business grows and evolves, it's important to consider diversifying your services to keep up with the changing demands of your customers and the industry. This can help you stay ahead of the competition and ensure the longevity of your business.

There are many ways to diversify your services, such as expanding your fleet to include different types of vehicles, offering new services such as delivery or storage, or even branching out into new geographical areas.

When considering diversifying your services, it's important to think about what your customers are looking for and what your strengths are as a business. Do you have the resources and expertise to expand into a new area, or is it better to focus on improving your existing offerings?

Once you've decided on the areas you want to diversify into, it's time to start researching and planning. This may include market research to determine the demand for the new services, developing a marketing strategy to reach your target audience, and investing in the necessary equipment and personnel.

It's important to take your time when diversifying your services. Don't rush into anything without fully understanding the potential risks and rewards. Remember, diversification is a gradual process and you can always adjust your plans as you go along.

At the end of the day, diversifying your services can bring new opportunities and help you grow your business in ways you never thought possible. So don't be afraid to step outside of your comfort zone and try something new!

Chapter 28. Building a Strong Online Presence

In today's digital age, having a strong online presence is crucial for any business, especially a transportation business. Not only does a well-designed website make it easy for customers to find you and learn about your services, but it also shows that your business is professional and trustworthy. In this chapter, we'll explore the steps you can take to build a strong online presence for your transportation business.

First and foremost, you'll need a website. A website is your online storefront, and it should be easy to navigate, informative, and visually appealing. When choosing a website builder, look for one that's user-friendly, affordable, and offers the features you need, such as the ability to accept online bookings and payments.

Next, make sure your website is optimized for search engines. This means using keywords related to your business in your website content and meta tags, as well as making sure your site is mobile-friendly and has a fast loading speed. By optimizing your website, you'll make it easier for customers to find you when searching for transportation services online.

In addition to a website, you should also have a strong social media presence. Choose the platforms that your target audience is most likely to use, such as Facebook, Twitter, or Instagram, and create a strategy for posting content that will engage your followers and build brand awareness. Consider sharing photos of your vehicles, offering special promotions, and answering customer questions on social media.

Finally, don't overlook the importance of online reviews. Encourage satisfied customers to leave reviews on platforms like Google, TripAdvisor, and Yelp. Positive reviews will not only help you attract new customers, but they also show that your business is trustworthy and professional. Respond to any negative reviews with a friendly and professional attitude, and work to resolve any issues the customer may have had.

Building a strong online presence takes time and effort, but it's well worth it in the long run. By following these tips, you'll be able to reach more customers, build your brand, and grow your transportation business.

Chapter 29. Customer Retention

Starting and growing a transportation business can be a long and challenging journey, but nothing is more rewarding than having loyal customers who choose your business time and time again. In this chapter, we'll dive into the importance of customer retention and the strategies you can implement to keep your customers coming back.

Why is customer retention important?

Retaining customers is crucial to the success of your transportation business. For starters, it's less expensive to retain existing customers than it is to acquire new ones. According to research, it costs five times more to acquire a new customer than it does to retain an existing one. So, if you're looking to save money and maximize your profits, retaining your current customers should be a top priority.

In addition, loyal customers tend to spend more, and they're also more likely to recommend your business to others. A referral from a satisfied customer can be worth more than any form of advertising. With customer retention, you'll be able to build a strong and consistent customer base, which will provide you with a stable source of income for years to come.

Strategies for customer retention

1. Provide exceptional customer service: One of the most effective ways to retain customers is by providing exceptional customer service. Make sure your customers are happy with the service they receive from your business, and go above and beyond to resolve any

issues they may have. Respond to customer inquiries in a timely manner and be proactive in addressing any concerns they may have.

2. Offer loyalty rewards: Another way to retain customers is by offering loyalty rewards. Offer incentives such as discounts, special promotions, or even a rewards program to show your appreciation for your customers' loyalty.

3. Personalize your approach: Personalization is key when it comes to retaining customers. Make your customers feel special and appreciated by sending them personalized emails, messages, or even thank-you notes. Personalizing your approach can help build trust and create a strong connection with your customers.

4. Ask for feedback: Finally, ask your customers for feedback and listen to what they have to say. This can help you identify any areas where you can improve and make changes to your business that will better meet your customers' needs.

In conclusion, customer retention is a crucial aspect of any transportation business. By implementing effective customer retention strategies, you'll be able to build a strong and loyal customer base, which will help you grow your business and increase your profits in the long run.

Chapter 30. Quality Control – The Key to Long-Term Success

Quality control is a critical component of any successful transportation business. It is what sets your business apart from the competition and sets the standard for customer satisfaction. By ensuring that your fleet is well-maintained, your operations are efficient, and your customer service is top-notch, you can establish a reputation for excellence that will keep your customers coming back for more.

So, how do you go about establishing a quality control program for your transportation business? Here are some tips to get you started:

1. Define your standards. Before you can start monitoring quality, you need to have a clear idea of what you are looking for. Determine what constitutes excellent service, safety, and efficiency, and then use these standards as the basis for your quality control program.

2. Train your employees. Your employees are the front line of your quality control program, so it is essential that they know what is expected of them. Provide training sessions to help them understand your standards and how to meet them.

3. Establish a system for monitoring quality. Whether it's through regular inspections, customer feedback, or something else, create a system that allows you to regularly check the quality of your operations.

4. Use technology to your advantage. There are many tools and technologies available that can help you monitor quality, such as GPS tracking systems, fleet management software, and customer feedback tools. Utilize these resources to gain a better understanding of your operations and identify areas for improvement.

5. Reward your employees for their hard work. When employees see that their hard work is appreciated, they are more likely to strive for excellence. Consider offering incentives such as bonuses, time off, or recognition programs to reward your employees for meeting or exceeding quality standards.

Quality control is an ongoing process, so be prepared to make changes and improvements as needed. By establishing a strong quality control program and continuously monitoring your operations, you can ensure that your transportation business is delivering the best possible service to your customers.

Chapter 31. Professional Development

As a transportation business owner, it's important to constantly strive for growth and improvement. One of the ways to do this is by continuing your own professional development. This can take many forms, from attending conferences and workshops, to taking courses and earning certifications.

The benefits of professional development are numerous. For one, it can help you stay up-to-date with the latest industry trends and advancements. It can also provide you with new insights and ideas, which can help you improve your business operations and bottom line. Additionally, investing in your own professional development can demonstrate to your employees that you are committed to your business, and can help to motivate and inspire them.

When choosing professional development opportunities, consider what areas of your business you would like to improve upon. For example, if you would like to enhance your marketing skills, consider attending a workshop or taking a course in digital marketing. Or, if you are looking to improve your leadership abilities, consider attending a leadership conference or taking a course in management.

Another option for professional development is mentorship. Find someone in your industry who has the experience and skills that you admire and reach out to them for guidance and advice. A mentor can help you navigate the challenges you may face as a business owner, and provide valuable insights and perspectives.

In summary, professional development is a crucial component of any successful transportation business. Whether you attend workshops, take courses, or seek out mentorship, investing in yourself and your business will pay off in the long run.

Chapter 32. Customer Feedback

Customer Feedback - Building Relationships and Improving Your Services

As a transportation business owner, it's important to understand what your customers need and want. This is where customer feedback comes into play. Listening to your customers and taking their feedback seriously is an essential part of improving your business and growing your customer base.

There are many ways to gather customer feedback. You can ask them directly through surveys, email or phone calls. You can also use online review sites like Yelp, TripAdvisor or Google Reviews to gather feedback. It's important to make sure you ask for feedback regularly and respond to it promptly. This shows your customers that you care about their opinions and are taking steps to improve your services.

Customer feedback can provide valuable insights into areas where you can improve your services. For example, if you consistently receive feedback about long wait times for pick-ups, you may need to invest in more vehicles or hire more drivers to reduce wait times. Similarly, if customers complain about rude or unprofessional drivers, you may need to provide more training or re-evaluate your hiring process.

It's important to not only listen to feedback but to act on it as well. If you implement changes based on customer feedback, let your customers know. This shows that you're taking their opinions seriously and working to improve their experience.

In addition to improving your services, customer feedback can also help you build stronger relationships with your customers. When you listen to and respond to their feedback, you show them that you value their opinions and care about their satisfaction. This can lead to increased customer loyalty and a larger customer base in the long run.

In conclusion, customer feedback is an important tool for improving your transportation business. Make sure to gather it regularly, respond to it promptly and act on it to build stronger relationships with your customers and improve your services.

Chapter 33. Partnering with Other Businesses

Starting a transportation business can be a challenging process, but it's a lot easier when you have a team of like-minded people working with you. This is where partnering with other businesses can be extremely beneficial. Whether it's a supplier, vendor, or another transportation company, having a strong network of business partners can help you achieve your goals faster and with greater success.

One of the biggest advantages of partnering with other businesses is that it can provide you with a steady stream of new customers. By partnering with a company that already has an established customer base, you can tap into that market and expand your own customer base. This can be especially useful if you're starting a transportation business in an unfamiliar market.

Another advantage of partnering with other businesses is that it can help you access resources and knowledge that you might not have access to otherwise. For example, if you partner with a company that specializes in transportation technology, you can benefit from their expertise and experience in that area. This can help you improve your operations, reduce costs, and become more competitive in the market.

Of course, partnering with other businesses is not without its risks. You need to be careful when choosing your business partners and make sure that you're working with a reputable company. You should also make sure that you have a clear understanding of the terms of the partnership and that you're comfortable with the level of commitment required.

When it comes to partnering with other businesses, it's important to remember that the goal is to work together to achieve a common goal. You want to find a partner that complements your skills and resources, and that shares your vision for the future. When you find the right partner, you'll be able to build a strong and mutually beneficial relationship that will help you grow your transportation business for years to come.

Chapter 34. Managing Growth

Starting a transportation business is a big step and it's even more exciting when your business starts to grow! As your business grows, it's important to have a plan in place to manage the growth. With proper planning, you can ensure that your business continues to grow in a sustainable and profitable way.

The first step in managing growth is to set clear goals for your business. What do you want to achieve in the short term and the long term? What are your priorities? Having a clear vision of what you want to achieve will help you make informed decisions about how to grow your business.

Next, you need to develop a plan for managing growth. This could involve expanding your fleet, hiring more employees, or diversifying your services. Whatever your plan may be, it's important to have a roadmap in place that outlines the steps you need to take to achieve your goals.

It's also important to invest in your infrastructure to support growth. This could involve updating your equipment, upgrading your technology, or improving your operations. Investing in your infrastructure will help you handle the increased demand as your business grows.

Another key factor in managing growth is to have a strong team in place. As your business grows, you'll need to rely on your employees more and more. Make sure you have a team in place that is motivated, skilled, and committed to helping your business succeed.

Finally, you need to be flexible and adaptable. The transportation industry is constantly changing and you need to be able to change with it. Stay informed about industry trends, be open to new ideas, and be willing to pivot when necessary.

In conclusion, managing growth is a crucial part of running a successful transportation business. With clear goals, a solid plan, strong infrastructure, and a great team, you can ensure that your business continues to grow and thrive for many years to come.

Chapter 35. Evaluating Your Business

Congratulations! You've made it this far, and your transportation business is up and running. But the journey doesn't end here. Just like any other business, you need to continuously evaluate and assess your performance to ensure you're heading in the right direction.

Evaluating your business allows you to identify areas of strength and opportunities for improvement, which can help you make informed decisions to drive growth and success.

Here are some key areas to focus on when evaluating your transportation business:

1. Financial performance: Take a closer look at your income statement, balance sheet, and cash flow statement to understand how your business is performing financially. You can then use this information to make informed decisions about how to allocate resources and manage expenses.

2. Customer satisfaction: Ask your customers for feedback on the services they've received. You can conduct surveys, use online review platforms, or simply ask for customer feedback directly. You can then use this information to make improvements and better meet customer needs.

3. Employee satisfaction: Ask your employees how they feel about working for your business. Ask them about their job satisfaction, what they enjoy about working for your business, and what they think could be improved. You can then use this information to make changes that will help employees feel valued and motivated.

4. Market trends: Stay up-to-date with the latest trends in the transportation industry. Evaluate your competition, identify new

opportunities, and make adjustments as needed to stay ahead of the curve.

5. Technology: Assess the technology you're using and evaluate whether there are any new technologies that could help you improve your operations and meet customer needs more effectively.

6. Brand image: Evaluate your brand image and see if there's anything you can do to improve it. Consider things like your logo, your website, and the way you interact with customers.

7. Compliance: Make sure you're meeting all of your legal obligations and adhering to industry standards and regulations.

Evaluating your business on a regular basis will help you stay on track and make informed decisions that drive growth and success. So don't be afraid to take a step back, assess your performance, and make any necessary changes. Your transportation business will be better for it.

Chapter 36. Preparing for the Future

Congratulations, you've made it this far! By now, you've learned a great deal about how to start and run a successful transportation business. But the journey doesn't stop here. As with any business, there will always be challenges and opportunities for growth and improvement. That's why it's important to always be thinking ahead and preparing for the future.

In this chapter, we'll go over some tips for making sure your transportation business stays ahead of the curve and continues to grow for years to come.

1. Stay Up-to-Date on Industry Trends

The transportation industry is constantly evolving, with new technologies and innovations emerging all the time. To stay competitive, it's important to stay up-to-date on the latest trends and changes in the industry. This could mean attending industry conferences, reading industry publications, or reaching out to other transportation business owners for their insights and advice.

2. Keep Your Fleet Modern

One of the biggest expenses for any transportation business is the cost of vehicles and equipment. By keeping your fleet modern and up-to-date, you'll be better positioned to compete in the marketplace and offer the best possible service to your customers. This could mean investing in new vehicles or upgrading existing ones with the latest technologies and features.

3. Plan for Future Expansion

As your business grows and becomes more successful, you may find that you need to expand in order to keep up with demand. Whether that means adding more vehicles to your fleet, hiring additional employees, or opening new locations, it's important to plan ahead for this growth so that you're ready when the time comes.

4. Diversify Your Services

One way to stay ahead of the competition and increase your revenue is to diversify your services. This could mean offering new types of transportation, such as delivery services or airport transportation, or expanding into new geographic areas. By offering a wide range of services, you'll be able to attract a wider range of customers and build a more sustainable business.

5. Invest in Your Team

Your employees are the backbone of your transportation business, and investing in their training, development, and well-being is essential for long-term success. Whether that means offering regular training sessions, promoting from within, or offering competitive benefits packages, taking care of your team will pay off in the form of increased productivity and loyalty.

6. Keep Your Business Plan Flexible

Finally, it's important to remember that no matter how well you plan, things can change quickly in the business world. That's why it's important to keep your business plan flexible and adaptable, so that you can pivot and make changes as needed. This could mean adjusting your goals, revising your marketing strategies, or investing in new technologies.

In conclusion, preparing for the future is all about staying flexible, staying ahead of the curve, and investing in your business, your team, and your customers. By following these tips, you'll be well on your way to continued success and growth in the transportation industry.

Chapter 37. Developing a Succession Plan

Starting a transportation business is a big accomplishment, but it's important to think about what will happen to the business once you're ready to retire or move on to something else. Developing a succession plan is a critical part of ensuring the longevity of your business and ensuring its success in the long-term.

A succession plan is essentially a roadmap for passing your business on to someone else. This could be a family member, a trusted employee, or even a third party. The key is to make sure that the transition is as smooth and seamless as possible so that your business continues to thrive even after you're no longer at the helm.

Here are some key steps to consider when developing your succession plan:

1. Identify your goals: Before you start making any concrete plans, it's important to identify your goals for the future of your business. Do you want to pass it on to your family? Do you want to sell it to someone else? Do you want to retire completely? Knowing your goals will help you determine what type of succession plan is right for you.

2. Assess your business: Take a good look at your business and determine what is working well and what needs improvement. This will help you identify any areas that need to be addressed before you pass the business on to someone else.

3. Choose your successor: Once you know your goals, you can start thinking about who would be the best fit to take over your business. Consider factors such as experience, skills, and passion for the business when making your decision.

4. Start training your successor: If you've identified a family member or employee who will be taking over your business, start training them now. Give them opportunities to learn about the business and work with you so that they are well-equipped to take over when the time comes.

5. Create a timeline: Develop a timeline for your succession plan so that you know when each step will occur. This will help you stay on track and make sure that everything is in place when you're ready to pass the business on.

6. Get legal advice: Consult with a lawyer or an accountant to make sure that your succession plan is legally sound. They can help you with issues such as transferring ownership, taxes, and any other legal considerations.

7. Review and revise: Regularly review and revise your succession plan to make sure that it's still in line with your goals and the current state of your business.

Developing a succession plan can be a daunting task, but it's an important step in ensuring the long-term success of your transportation business. By planning ahead and working with the right people, you can make the transition as smooth and stress-free as possible, leaving your business in good hands for years to come.

Chapter 38. Emerging Trends in the Industry

Starting a transportation business can be an exciting journey, but it can also be a bit intimidating when it comes to staying ahead in a constantly evolving industry. To remain competitive and maintain a strong reputation, it's essential to stay up to date with the latest trends and advancements in the field. In this chapter, we'll explore some of the emerging trends that are shaping the transportation industry and discuss how you can stay ahead of the game.

1. Embracing Technology: Technology is playing a more significant role in the transportation industry than ever before. From GPS tracking to telematics, technology is helping companies to streamline their operations, reduce costs, and provide a more efficient service to their customers. Investing in the latest technology can give your business an edge and help you stay ahead of the competition.

2. Sustainability: Consumers and businesses alike are becoming increasingly environmentally conscious, and the transportation industry is no exception. Companies are looking for ways to reduce their carbon footprint and make their operations more sustainable. This can include investing in electric or hybrid vehicles, reducing emissions, and implementing environmentally friendly practices.

3. On-demand Services: On-demand services have become increasingly popular in recent years, and the

transportation industry is no exception. Companies are now offering on-demand services such as ride-sharing and food delivery. This trend is expected to continue to grow, and businesses that offer on-demand services are likely to find success in the coming years.

4. Autonomous Vehicles: Autonomous vehicles are becoming a reality, and they're set to revolutionize the transportation industry. From self-driving trucks to autonomous delivery vehicles, these advancements are expected to have a significant impact on the industry. While the transition to autonomous vehicles may be challenging, it's essential to stay ahead of the game and be prepared for the changes that are coming.

5. Big Data: Big data is playing a big role in the transportation industry, and companies are using data to make informed decisions and improve their operations. From tracking shipments to analyzing customer behavior, data can help businesses to optimize their operations, reduce costs, and provide a better service to their customers.

In conclusion, the transportation industry is undergoing significant changes, and it's essential to stay up to date with the latest trends and advancements. Whether it's embracing technology, focusing on sustainability, or exploring new business models, the key to success is to be adaptable and stay ahead of the game. By keeping an eye on emerging trends and being open to new ideas, you can ensure that your transportation business remains competitive and continues to grow and thrive.

Chapter 39. Best Practices for Success

Starting a transportation business is a big step, and it can be overwhelming at times. But don't worry! With the right tools, resources, and knowledge, you can turn your business into a success story. In this chapter, we'll go over some of the best practices you can use to help you achieve your goals and reach new heights.

1. Prioritize Safety

Your top priority should always be the safety of your customers, employees, and vehicles. Make sure that you have all the necessary safety equipment in place, including seat belts, fire extinguishers, and GPS tracking devices. In addition, ensure that your vehicles are regularly maintained to ensure that they are in top working order.

2. Set Realistic Goals

Setting realistic goals is crucial for success in any business. When it comes to your transportation business, make sure that your goals are achievable and realistic. For example, if you are starting a small business, it may be unrealistic to expect to achieve the same growth rate as a large corporation. Instead, focus on setting goals that are achievable for your business size and structure.

3. Invest in Marketing

Marketing is a critical component of any business, and your transportation business is no exception. Make sure that you have a solid marketing plan in place, and invest in advertising and promotions to reach your target audience. This can include online advertising, direct mail, email marketing, and more.

4. Network and Collaborate

Networking and collaborating with other businesses can help you grow your business and expand your reach. Consider partnering with local hotels, restaurants, and other transportation companies to cross-promote your services and reach new customers. In addition, attend industry events and conferences to connect with other business owners and learn about the latest trends and best practices.

5. Utilize Technology

Technology is changing the transportation industry at a rapid pace, and it's important to stay up-to-date with the latest innovations. This can include using GPS tracking and dispatch software to optimize your operations, as well as offering online booking and payment options for your customers.

6. Focus on Customer Service

Customer service is key to the success of your transportation business. Make sure that you provide a high-quality experience for your customers, from start to finish. This can include offering flexible scheduling, comfortable vehicles, and professional drivers. In addition, provide excellent customer support and respond promptly to any customer concerns or issues.

7. Continuously Evaluate Your Business

Evaluating your business on a regular basis is important for growth and success. Take the time to review your financials, customer feedback, and employee satisfaction regularly to identify areas for improvement. Based on this information, make any necessary changes to your business plan and strategies to ensure that you are on the right track.

In conclusion, the best practices for success in the transportation industry are wide-ranging and include a focus on safety, goal-setting, marketing, networking, technology utilization, customer service, continuous evaluation, and more. By incorporating these best practices into your business plan and operations, you can build a strong foundation for long-term success and growth.

Chapter 40. Conclusion

Congratulations, you've made it to the end of your journey in starting and growing your transportation business! By now, you should have a clear understanding of the various aspects involved in running a successful transportation business.

Starting a transportation business is a big decision, and it can be a challenging journey, but with dedication, hard work, and a willingness to learn, you can achieve your goals. By following the steps outlined in this book, you'll be on the path to success in no time.

It's important to remember that there's no one right way to run a transportation business. What works for one business might not work for another, so always be open to new ideas and strategies. And don't be afraid to ask for help. There are many resources available to help you along the way, including industry associations, business mentors, and local organizations.

As you move forward with your transportation business, make sure you stay focused on your goals, continue to learn and grow, and always strive to provide the best possible service to your customers. With these principles in mind, there's no limit to what you can achieve.

So go out there and make your mark in the transportation industry. Best of luck to you!

Bonus

here's a list of some tips for success in your transportation business:

1. Maintain a strong, ethical reputation by providing quality services and treating all customers and employees with respect.

2. Continuously educate yourself and your team on industry updates and advancements.

3. Focus on customer satisfaction by actively seeking feedback and implementing changes to improve your services.

4. Build strong relationships with your partners and suppliers to ensure smooth operations and access to quality resources.

5. Stay organized and keep detailed records of your operations to easily track your progress and identify areas for improvement.

6. Foster a positive, collaborative work environment by encouraging open communication and promoting employee growth and development.

7. Be proactive in managing costs and finding ways to maximize efficiency in your operations.

8. Stay up-to-date on relevant regulations and standards to ensure compliance and maintain a safe, responsible business.

9. Continuously evaluate and adjust your strategies as needed to ensure long-term success.

10. Maintain a strong online presence through active social media, marketing efforts, and search engine optimization.

Remember, success in your transportation business requires hard work, dedication, and a willingness to adapt to changes in the industry. Keep these tips in mind and stay focused on your goals to see continued growth and success in your business.

Congratulations, you have now completed this book on starting and managing a transportation business! We hope that you have found the information and guidance within these pages to be valuable and informative, and that you feel confident and well-equipped to launch and grow your business.

As you embark on this exciting journey, we wish you all the best in your endeavors. May your business be successful, your customers satisfied, and your growth steady. May you find joy and fulfillment in your work, and may your business bring you financial security and stability.

Remember, running a transportation business can be challenging, but it can also be incredibly rewarding. Trust in yourself and your abilities, be persistent and dedicated, and don't be afraid to ask for help when you need it. With hard work and determination, we are sure that you will achieve great things.

We wish you all the best, and all the success in the world. Happy travels!

www.ingramcontent.com/pod-product-compliance
Lightning Source LLC
Chambersburg PA
CBHW071054290526
45795CB00004B/1477